Jacob of Sarug's Homily on Paul's Word to Seek What is Above and on Outer Darkness

Texts from Christian Late Antiquity

76

Series Editor

George Anton Kiraz

TeCLA (Texts from Christian Late Antiquity) is a series presenting ancient Christian texts both in their original languages and with accompanying contemporary English translations.

Jacob of Sarug's Homily on Paul's Word to Seek What is Above and on Outer Darkness

Edited and Translated by

Dominique Sirgy

2022

Gorgias Press LLC, 954 River Road, Piscataway, NJ, 08854, USA

www.gorgiaspress.com

Copyright © 2022 by Gorgias Press LLC

All rights reserved under International and Pan-American Copyright Conventions. No part of this publication may be reproduced, stored in a retrieval system or transmitted in any form or by any means, electronic, mechanical, photocopying, recording, scanning or otherwise without the prior written permission of Gorgias Press LLC.

2022

ISBN 978-1-4632-4464-4   **ISSN 1935-6846**

Library of Congress Cataloging-in-Publication Data

A Cataloging-in-Publication Record is available from the Library of Congress.

Printed in the United States of America

TABLE OF CONTENTS

Table of Contents v
Acknowledgments vii
Introduction 1
Text and Translation 7
    Memra 105 On that Word that Paul the Apostle said:
        'Seek what is Above… and Think about What is
        Above', and on Outer Darkness 8
Bibliography 45
Index of Biblical References 47

Acknowledgments

The present homily was translated with indispensable revisions by Sebastian Brock and Dayroyo Antonios Gharib, to both of whom I am very grateful. The translation began during the first lockdown of Covid 2020, when George Kiraz sent out an announcement about the opportunity to translate Jacob of Serugh's homilies. I have deeply appreciated the chance to escape the challenge of these times amid the verses of Jacob's metrical homilies.

INTRODUCTION

> INFORMATION ON THIS HOMILY
> Homily Title: On that Word that Paul the Apostle said: 'Seek what is Above… and Think about What is Above', and on Outer Darkness
> Source of Text: *Homiliae Selectae Mar-Jacobi Sarugensis*, edited by Paul Bedjan (Paris-Leipzig: Harrassowitz, 1907, 2nd ed. Piscataway: Gorgias Press, 2006), vol. 3, pp. 876–892. [Homily 105]
> Lines: 344

Jacob of Sarug was born in Kurtam around 451 A.D. and trained at the School of Edessa. A gifted poet, Jacob followed in the tradition of Ephrem's (d. 373) symbolic theology, composing both liturgical texts and prose works. However, he is most recognized for his dodecasyllabic verse *memre*, more than 380 of which survive. The present homily "On that Word that Paul the Apostle said: 'Seek what is Above…and Think about What is Above', and on Outer Darkness," was written as a caution to listeners who prioritize worldly matters and forget their true home "above." Through frightful descriptions of Sheol's desolation, Jacob warns that concern with the temporal world leads to an afterlife remote from God and the possibility of repentance. Faith, love, God's mercy, and following the commandments are all means by which Jacob encourages Christians to escape a dismal fate. He relies on natural symbolism and the scriptures to teach the congregation about humankind's ultimate God-given purpose: to reside eternally in His glory.

After a short appeal to divine assistance to grant him suitable words for his *memre*—a common opening plea in Jacob's writings—the homily turns to the salvific instruction that the natural world provides to humans. Animals bow before man, the earth provides sustenance, the winds offer cold and heat. All the earth, Jacob intones, is subjugated to humans and honors them.[1] It does so because man is in the image of the Godhead.[2] This fact is made evident in humans' corporality, their straight build and their faces turned up towards the heavens. Yet, Jacob laments, humans do not take notice of their own glory and bend themselves as beasts towards the earth.[3] To redress their error, Jacob prods his audience to take counsel from nature and how plants reach towards the sky:

> You are implanted in the ground, [so] raise yourself from it
>   and do not remain there,
> Just as a tree that is planted in the ground and ascends
>   above.
> Let your body stand in the earth upon its dust,
> And your very mind be in the heights with God.[4]

The homily's natural symbolism is a popular feature of late antique Syriac literature,[5] where the visible world gives a glimpse into the invisible one by means of symbols, and where each symbol guides its observer toward the divine.[6] Jacob thus draws from natural symbolism to remind his congregation that they are strangers on earth and intended for heaven. They are thus encouraged to extend their minds up to their divinely-prepared home.

However, the capacity of the mind to "think about what is above," has limits in the homily. It is faith, rather, that spans the farthest reaches:

---

[1] Lines 5–58.
[2] Lines 52–53.
[3] Line 74.
[4] Lines 3–6.
[5] See, for instance, Sebastian Brock, *The Harp of the Spirit: Poems of Saint Ephrem the Syrian* (Cambridge: Aquila Books, 2013), 22.
[6] George Saber, "La Typologie Sacramentaire et Baptismale de Saint Ephrem," *Parole de l'Orient* 5, no. 1–2 (1973): 75, 80.

> Hither, the preacher of faith has sent you
> To the place where angels never ascended, nor even beheld.
> The mind fell short [of reaching] there as did speech and tongue,
> And faith was raised to the hidden place.[7]

Though the homily is based in the Pauline exhortation to "think about what is above," faith ascends past the reach of thought to arrive at the place of the Lord. Faith rises higher than all the spiritual assemblies to come to the dwelling of the Trinity in the Holy of Holies.[8] Surpassing the capacity of thought, faith, powered by love, is able to reach the Father: "The eye has not seen and the heart of man did not reckon … What the Father prepared for those who love what is above."[9]

The role of faith and love in bringing humans close to God in this homily resembles that which Jacob ascribes to prayer elsewhere. In his writings on prayer preserved in the Maronite manuscript British Library Add. 14535, Jacob writes how prayer grants access to the divine mysteries:

> Prayer reveals the profundities of the Divine,
> By it one enters to behold the mystery of hidden things.
> It is the key able to open all doors;
> From it one can clearly espy what is hidden,
> By it the soul can approach to speak with God,
> It raises up the mind so that it reaches the Majesty.[10]

Similar to the role of faith and love in the homily, prayer rises to the hidden place of the Lord to converse with Him.

Although the descriptions of faith, love, and prayer align in the homily and the excerpt on prayer, the texts' portrayals of the mind diverge. In the homily, the mind's reaches have limits

---

[7] Lines 151–154.
[8] Lines 165–168.
[9] Line 193–194.
[10] Sebastian Brock, "An Early Maronite Text on Prayer," *Parole de l'Orient* 13 (1986): 89.

whereas in the present excerpt, the mind is raised to God's majesty through prayer. Jacob was not a systematic thinker, and discrepancies between his writings can be detected. Nevertheless, the ascent to the Trinity's mysterious abode is a theme that emerges consistently in his writing.

Alongside heartening encouragement to seek the place of God, Jacob also employs stern admonishment to instruct his listeners. About one third of the homily is devoted to vivid descriptions of Sheol's darkness and isolation from the Lord: "The Lord of light is not there, so which light / Is able to descend and shine there without being corrupted?"[11] To avoid eternal damnation, Jacob implores his audience to repent before the moment of their death:

> Here the door of mercy is open before sinners,
> And it is easy for you to enter each day if you wish
> Seek mercy for yourself before the door is closed in front of
> > you,
> And you increase your cries when there is no one to answer
> > or hear you.[12]

During one's earthly life, repentance is readily accessible. But following death, the door of mercy closes on the souls in Sheol and their cries are no longer heard. It is therefore urgent for people to repent before the moment of death. Jacob reassures listeners that, so long as they willfully choose it, divine mercy will accept their repentance:

> A drop of mercy from that infinite sea,
> Is able to wash the iniquities of the world if you so will it.
> You do not desire to hinder [your] mercy from sinners,
> It is [their choice] to hinder mercy, for they did not seek
> > mercy.[13]

---

[11] Lines 117–118.
[12] Lines 287–288, 291–292.
[13] Lines 331–334.

No one, Jacob emphasizes, is responsible for impeding divine mercy, save those who do not seek it and choose the darkness of Sheol instead. But God's infinite mercy washes over those who wish for it through penitence. His homily thus exhorts listeners to contrition with the promise that it will meet with God's mercy.

The homily references biblical figures to provide listeners with a models for repentance. King David moistened his bed with tears and called to the Lord from his "whirlpool filled with sin."[14] He pled that he would not be counted among the sons of perdition[15] and he recognized that he was made in the image of God in order to glorify Him. Though he had descended deeply into sin, and "dissipated his goods on harlots and lechery,"[16] his repentance was readily met with God's mercy and love.

Jacob's "On that Word that Paul the Apostle said: 'Seek what is Above…and Think about What is Above', and on Outer Darkness," warns listeners about the consequences of rejecting God's plan for humankind. Throughout the text, Jacob expresses frustration with the worldly concerns of his congregation[17] and attempts to correct them by recalling the pains of Sheol and their divinely-prepared, heavenly abode. As a monk and preacher, he dutifully closes with a prayer on their behalf, "Oh, Good One, whose door of mercy is opened and [who] invites the wicked / Glory to you and mercy on us at all times."[18]

---

[14] Line 302.
[15] Lines 313.
[16] Line 340.
[17] Susan Ashbrook Harvey, "To Whom Did Jacob Preach?" in *Jacob of Serugh and His Times: Studies in Sixth-Century Syriac Christianity*, ed. George Kiraz (Piscataway: Gorgias Press, 2010), 118–119.
[18] Lines 343–344.

TEXT AND TRANSLATION

Memra 105

On that Word that Paul the Apostle said: 'Seek what is Above... and Think about What is Above', and on Outer Darkness

1   Lord of the heights who lowered his loftiness towards our evil,
       Lower your exalted Word towards us so that I may speak about you.
       All speeches, expressions and words are yours
       Because were it not through you, no one would be moved to speak to you.
5   Behold, all silent creatures speak to you,
       [With] distinct praises, not stopping glorifying you.
       Behold, the sky recounts your glory,[1] without ceasing,
       [This sky that is] the garment full of luminous windows of light.
       Behold, the empty [lower heavenly sphere] beneath, it praises you
10   With thunder, lighting, clouds, and winds circulating around it.
       Behold [the lower heavenly sphere] glorifies you with the flocks of fowl and birds,
       With their twittering and songs, it gives praise.
       The earth spread out and scattered soil at [the border] of the sea,
       Behold [the earth] sings hallelujah to you through its mountains, valleys and plains.[2]

---

[1] Cf. Psalm 19:1.
[2] Cf. Isaiah 42:5.

B876	: 1
	:
	: 5
	:
	:
	10
	:
	:

15	The forest thicket and animals that dwell therein [on earth],
	Behold, [the lower heavenly sphere] sends you great marvel and amazement.
	The water's abyss and all those swimming reptiles,
	Behold, [the water's abyss] extols you without ceasing from being amazed [by you].
	Behold, all creatures glorify you in their own manner,
20	Because they do not cease from the praise that is owed to you.
	It is fitting for us to glorify [you] on behalf of all the creatures,
	Which stand before us and serve us like maidservants.
	Behold, the whole world is subjugated to us by our Creator,
	The sky, the earth, the sea, the air, and all that is in them.
25	Your Lord granted you servants that stand and serve you,
	And as for a King, they make haste each day and honor you.
	Like maidservants, the sky and the earth stand before you,
	And though you do not command [them], each day they rush to your service.
	See the expanse and the luminaries as wax candles,
30	That the whole day carries to shine forth before you.
	The sky is holding up the light and standing before you like a handmaiden,
	So that you do not travel on your path in darkness, amid stumbling blocks.
	The air is poured out as though for your breath and it rears you,
	For without it, you would not even have an hour of life.

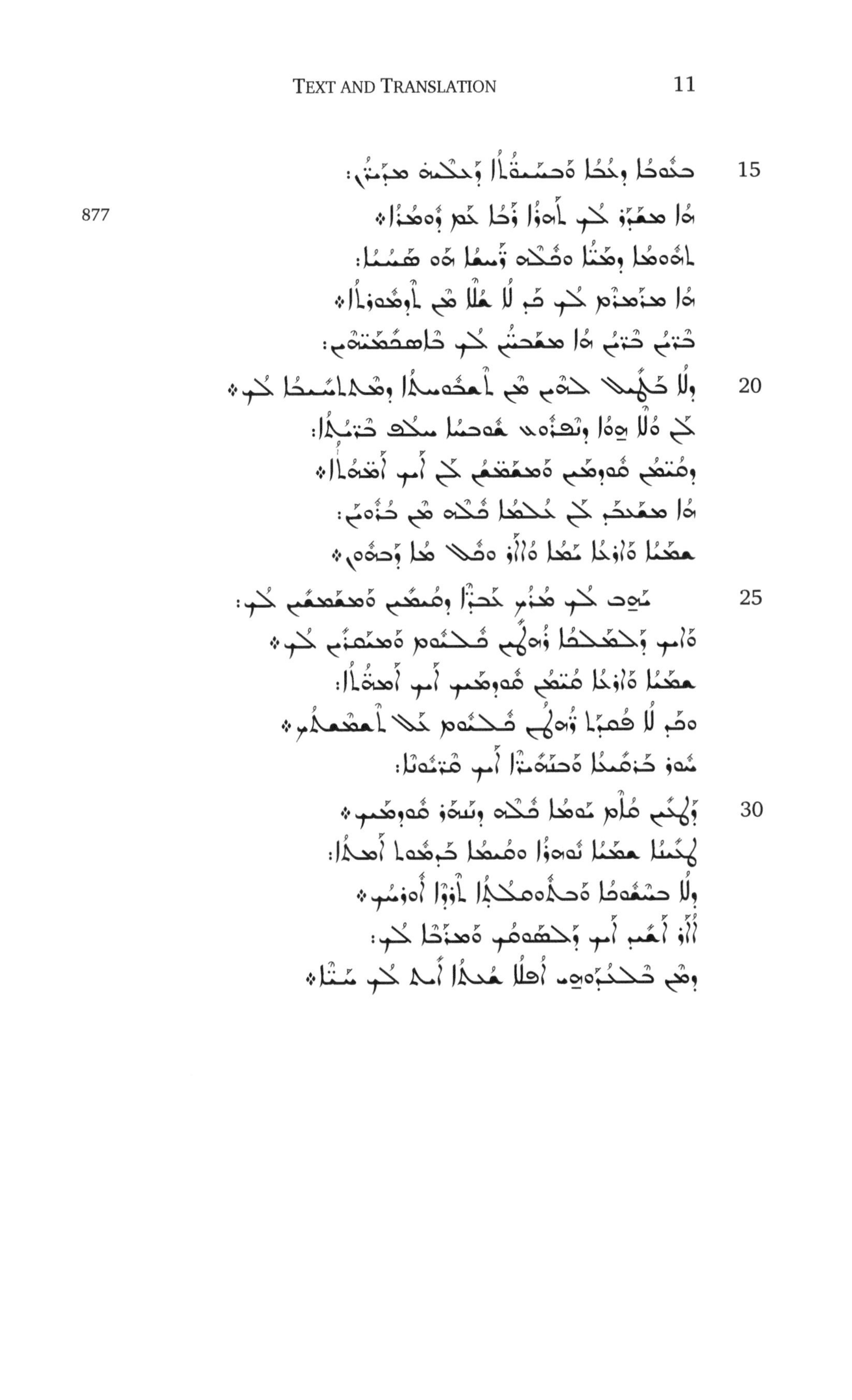

35	Behold, the cold and the heat are mixed in it,
	That, by its breath you can live a corporeal life.
	At times it cools and at times it warms and it rears you,
	Your life is sustained through its cold and heat.
	The earth is set firmly beneath your path and is watchful over you,
40	So that it does not swallow you up as it did Dathan and Abiram.[3]
	The earth is made like a maidservant and is bearing you:
	It disgorges and pushes out all plants for your sake.
	Behold, the trees bearing and standing for their foods.
	And each one of them in its time presents gifts before you.
45	Behold, the animals bent before you in their own forms:
	Offering you prostrate adoration as for a king.
	Behold, the bull who lowers his head and worships you,
	He does not hinder you from placing a yoke upon its shoulders.
	The donkey and the horse bend before you, as though for your seat,
50	In order to escort you in various places so that you might ascend and sit.
	The different races of all sorts of animals bow before you,
	For the great image of the Godhead is fashioned in you.
	The image of your Lord is depicted in your soul and your body is upright,
	In order that it not become bent like the animals who bow before you.

---

[3] Cf. Numbers 3.

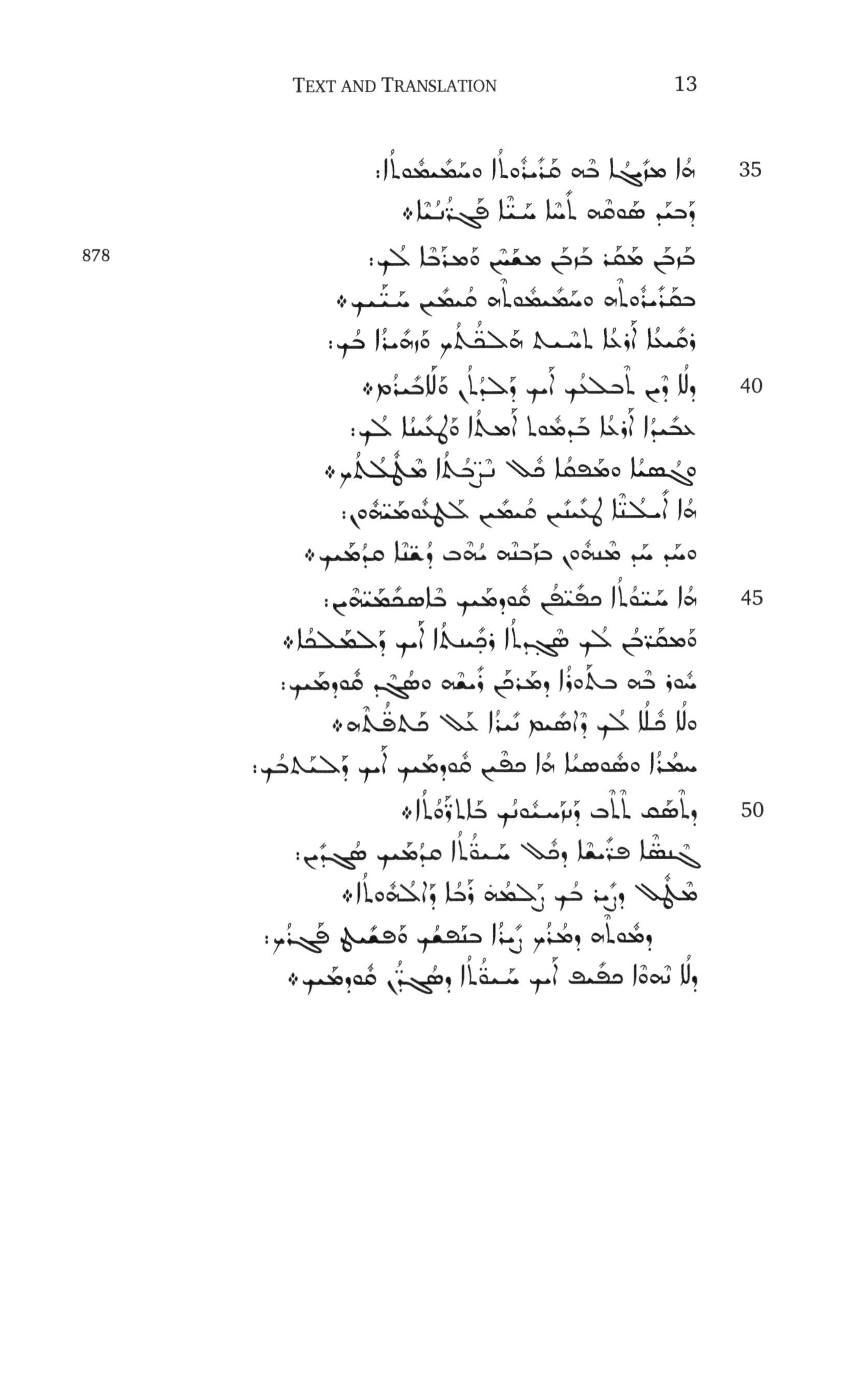

55	He straightened you, set you upright, and directed your face towards heaven,
	That you may see your place and consider how beautiful it is.
	He directed your face towards your place, the original one,
	For this land that you stand on is not yours.
	The form of your body cries out, that you are not earthly,
60	You are from above, seek the things which are above and contemplate them.
	You are a stranger and a foreigner in this place,
	Do not think about what is in it because it is not yours.
	Death comes, making what is yours no longer yours,
	and, like a plunderer, [it] separates and removes you from your possessions.
65	If [one's] need passes over the day's measure,
	It is a burden, in this case, and does not permit you to climb above.
	Do not gather for yourself the burden of the world and do not drown
	Your soul because the great image of the Godhead is depicted in it.
	You are that image of God, seek [therefore] what is above,
70	Do not lower yourself, seeking the earth like animals.
	This is a disgrace for the image of the king seeking the affairs of slaves,
	And brings oneself down from glory to contemptible disgrace.
	Why do you not take notice of your glory, oh man,
	For your head is not bent towards the ground like the animals.[4]

---

[4] Cf. Psalm 49:12 and 20.

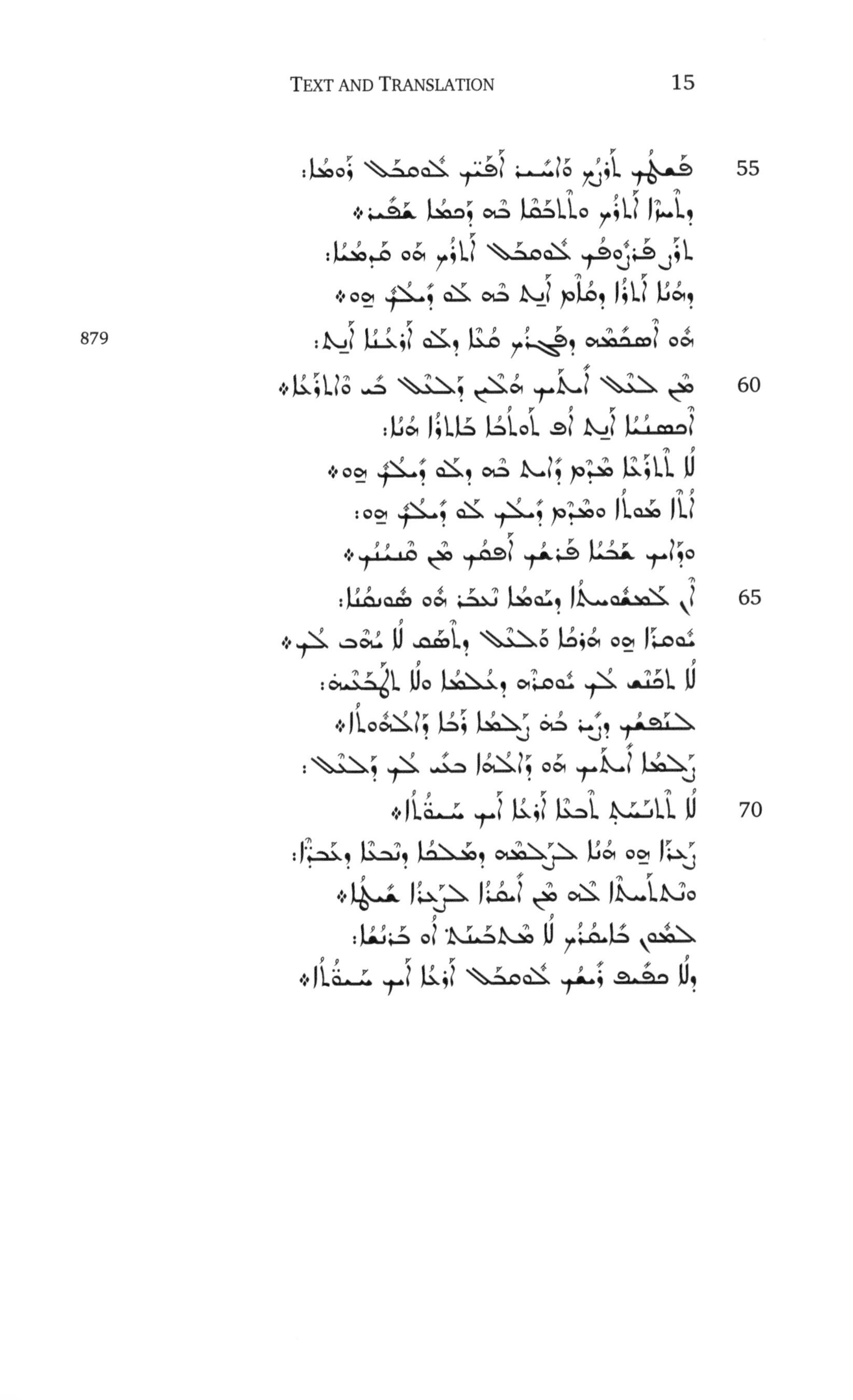

75 Why do you resemble a beast in your deeds,
    They are only pleased with what concerns the belly.
    Do not be like that one that is bent and bows before you,
    that you may not also submit yourself to the beast and resemble it.[5]
    Be a tree that, upright, ascends towards the heights,
80 Do not abide below, so that those who pass by do not cut you off.[6]
    The teaching is revealed to you through an earth's plant
    About how it ascends from within the soil to the heights above.
    It has no soul, nor even sense, yet ascends above
    Just as the Creator commanded from the beginning.
85 Behold, the upright plants ascending towards the heights,
    And your gaze turns to examine the things below!
    The plant rises from the deep to the heights of the air:
    And you seek to remain on the earth like a mole!
    Behold, the trees that leave the ground and ascend from it,
90 For it is beloved to them to be in the air's neighborhood.
    Look upon the tree that rends the earth and rises from it,
    So that it goes into the air to produce [its] leaves and fruits.
    There are one or two trees, if only it were possible
    That would stretch their branches as they rise to the stars.

---

[5] Ibid.
[6] Cf. Psalm 80:12–13.

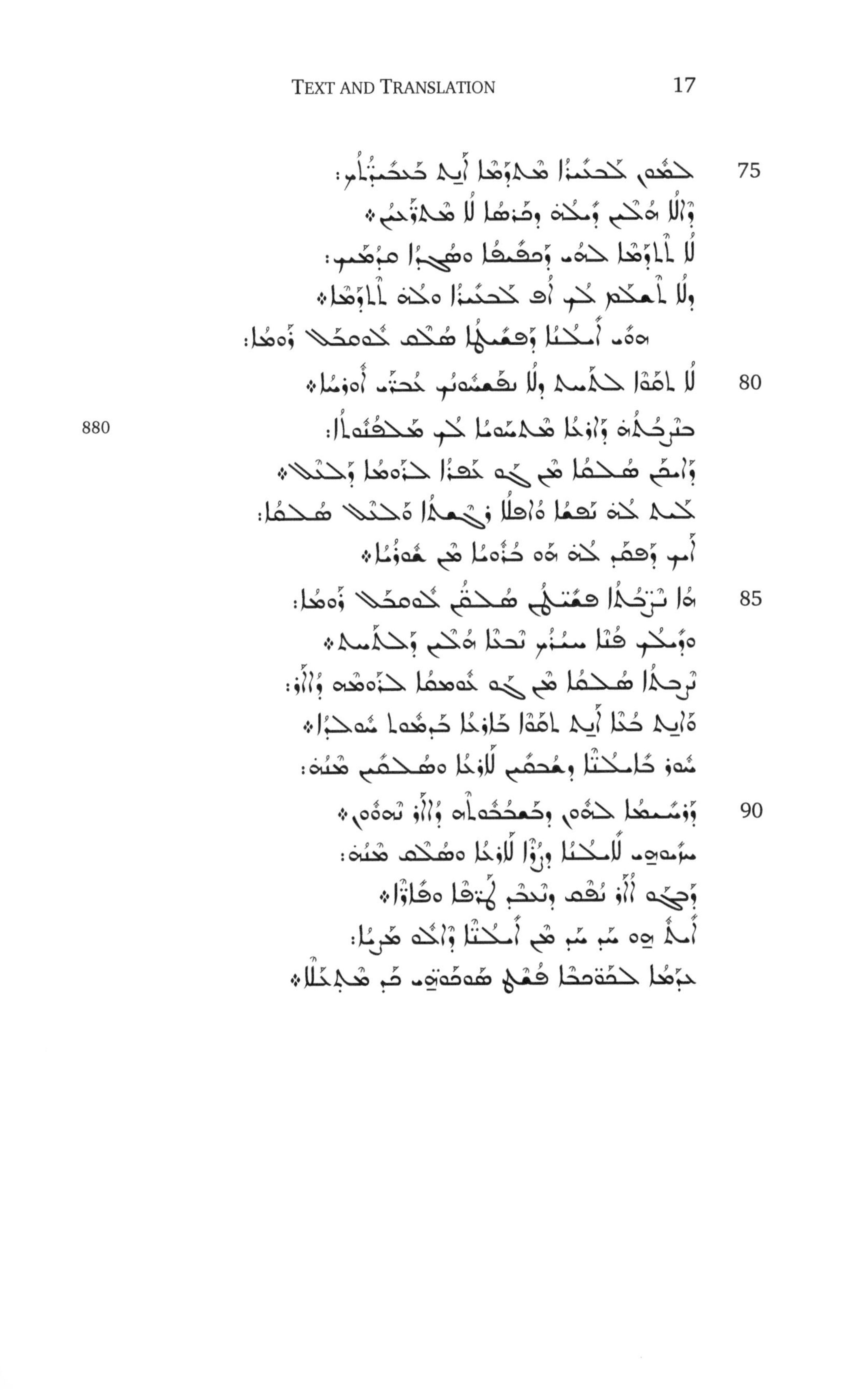

95   And because of this, whenever it is cut down and falls to the ground
There is no way for the water to submerge its lightness.
It becomes a vessel and flies in the air over the floods
Carrying a heavy weight and the great sea does not submerge it.
Because it left the weight of the earth and rose from it:
100   Whenever it falls upon streams, it is not drowned [by flowing waters].
Now, be also a tree whose roots within the depths
Are planted and whose head passes over above to the sky.
You are implanted in the ground, [so] raise yourself from it and do not remain there,
Just as a tree that is planted in the ground and ascends above.
105   Let your body stand in the earth upon its dust,
And your very mind be in the heights with God.
Extend your thoughts like branches towards virtues,
Make fruit whose perfume pleases the heavenly beings.
Be a bearer of righteousness and holiness,
110   Mercy and pure love that is free of deceit.
So that you may be a praiseworthy olive tree in the house of the Lord,[7]
And a just person who springs up like a palm tree.[8]
And [so that] whenever they cut you off from your roots[9] for a short time:
You may acquire wings above the world like an angel.

---

[7] Cf. Psalm 52:8.
[8] Cf. Psalm 92:12.
[9] Cf. Psalm 52:5; Matthew 7:19; and Luke 3:9.

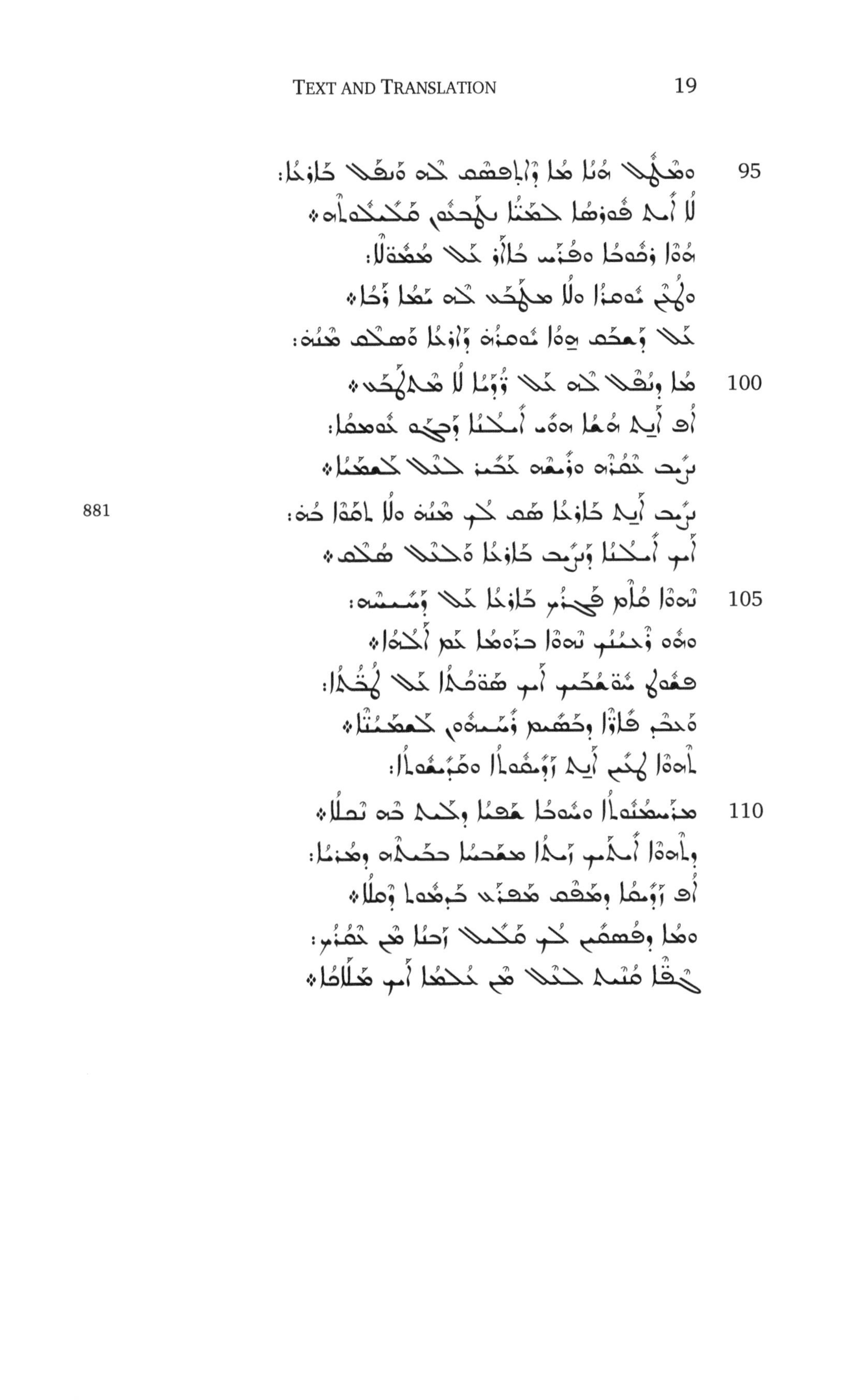

115	And when the evil powers endeavor to submerge you,
	They [themselves] drown but your lightness will not be forced to sink down.
	Your plant is fire and spirit from within the water
	Of baptism, [therefore] send the plant to the heights where it belongs.
	Leave the earth and do not look at it for it is full of harm,
120	Turn your gaze to the pleasant place that is above you.
	Behold, the sky coaxes you with its beauty to ascend towards it
	And see its light and all its fair forms.
	Do not fix your gaze on the place full of stumbling blocks,
	Make your mind fly to the limpid place that is above.
125	This place in which you stand is dark and gloomy,
	Hasten your course to the land of light that is above you.
	Behold, it is enticing you with the original door,
	To see the ineffable beauty behind it.
	The sky is adorned before you and showing you [the way],
130	The hosts are running and [thus] motivating you.
	Behold, the luminaries are suspended above you like fruits,
	[So that you may] ascend and pluck the great light and delight in it.
	The earth only shows her adornment in the month of April,
	And after a brief time it is spoiled as though it never was.

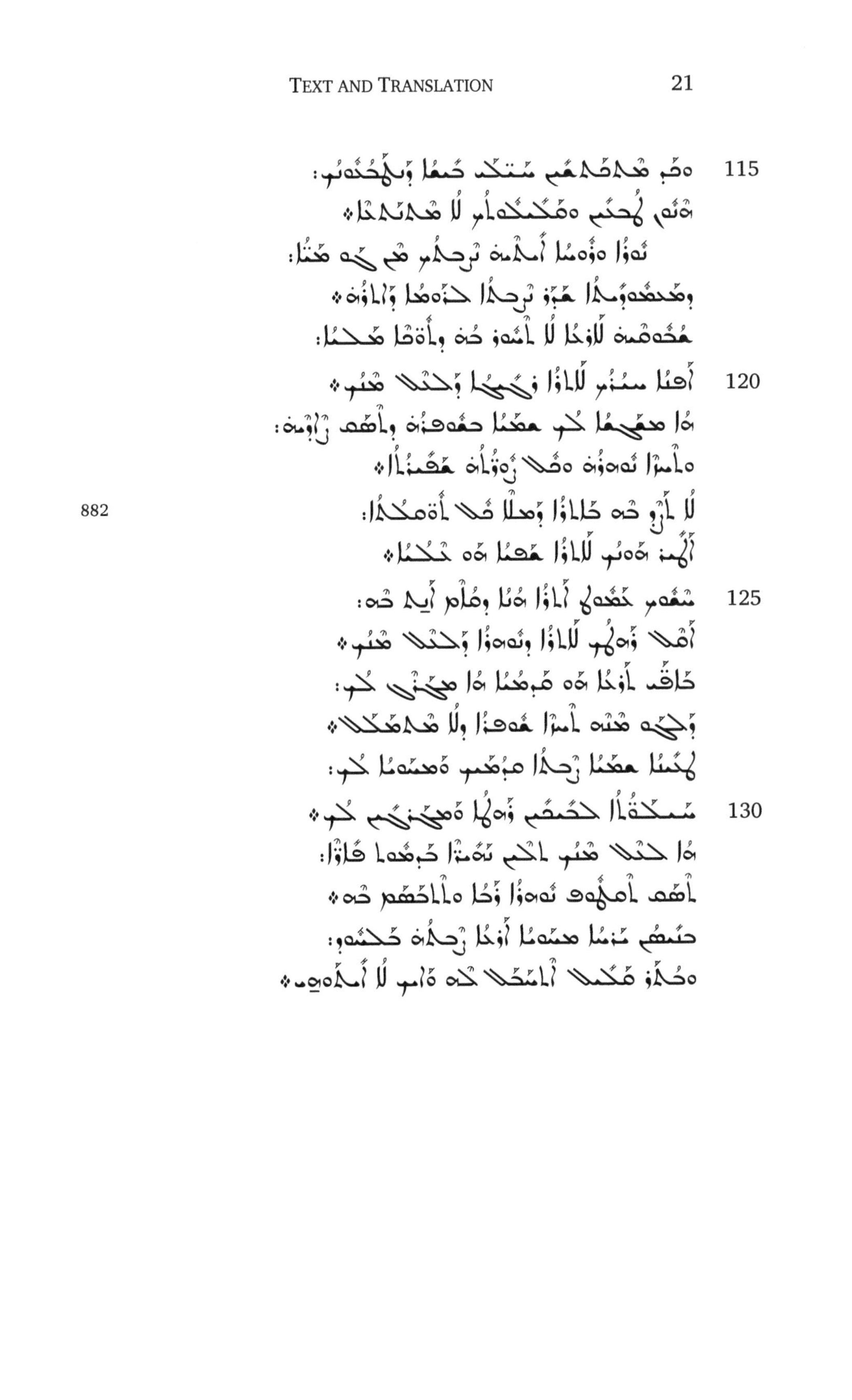

135　For a short time, she arranges and shows all her beauty,
　　And when you seek to be consoled by it, it burns up.
　　She adorns herself with [many] colors of buds and blossoms,
　　And whenever the sun warms, they tilt and are singed as by fire.
　　As with April, time granted you brief adornment,
140　Then death arrives, casted you into the earth, and destroyed your beauty.
　　Look upon the firmament, the habitation that extends over the uttermost regions,
　　Because time passes but its adornment does not wane.[10]
　　And this demonstrates to whomever sees lucidly,
　　That the desirable adornment that is above [the earth] is without alteration.
145　"Seek that which is above and contemplate," Paul cries out[11]
　　Because the place of light is your place, not the darkness.
　　The things which are above are life for whoever receives [of them],
　　And the things that are below are death for whoever seeks them.
　　Seek the things which are above and contemplate the place of your Lord,
150　[Where] Christ sits at the right [hand] in great glory.[12]
　　Hither, the preacher of faith has sent you
　　To the place where angels never ascended, nor even beheld.
　　The mind fell short [of reaching] there as did speech and tongue,
　　And faith was raised to the hidden place.

---

[10] Cf. Isaiah 40:22.
[11] Cf. Colossians 3:2.
[12] Cf. Colossians 3:1.

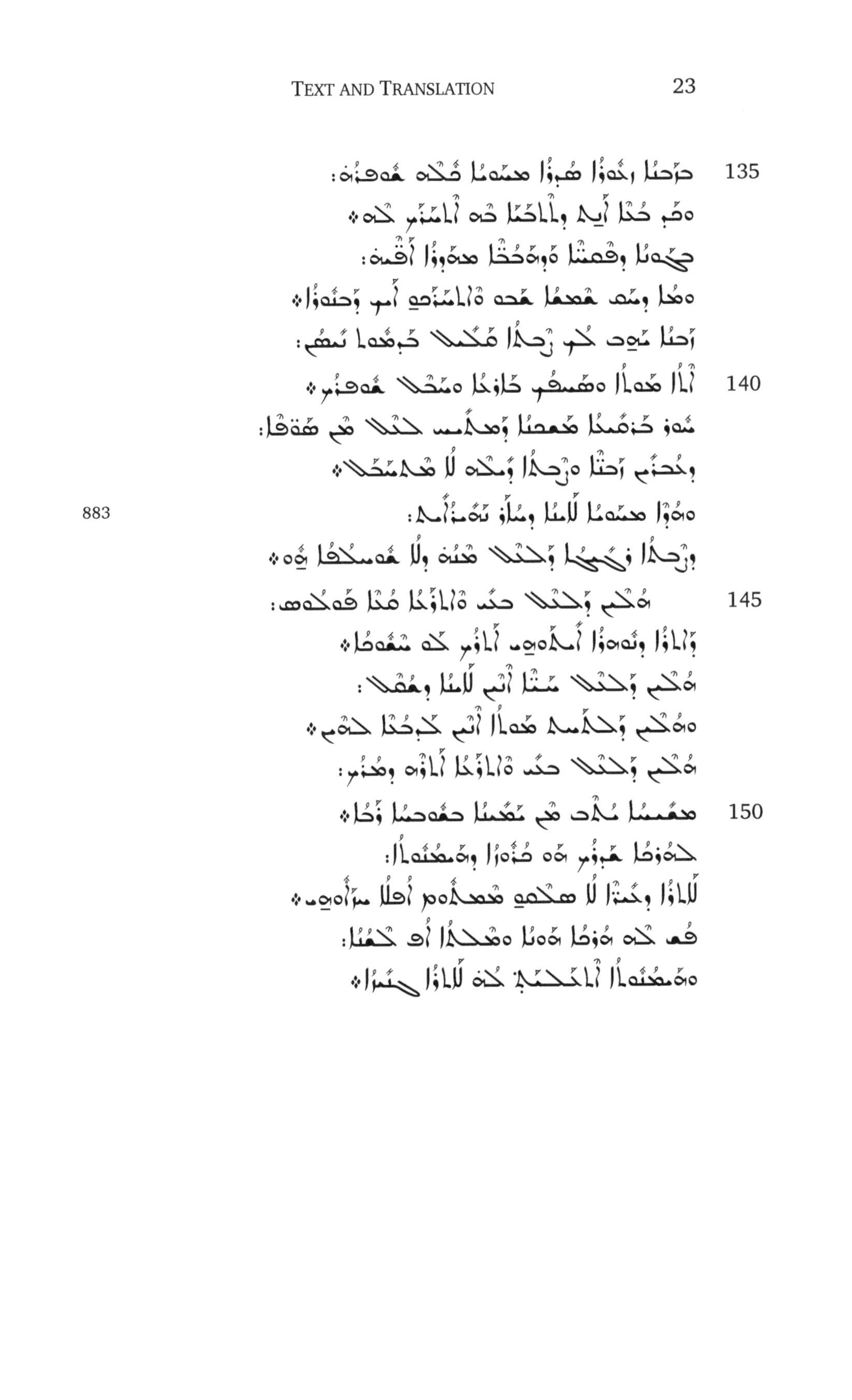

155　Faith did not desire to stand—not even near the angels,
　　 For she rushed to be lifted above them.
　　 She left the fiery assembles of the house of Gabriel behind her,
　　 And did not delay—not even by the legions of the house of Michael.
　　 She passed the hosts, the chiefs of hosts, and dominions,
160　She went beyond the spiritual principalities, authorities, and all the powers.[13]
　　 She made haste and leapt [over] the choirs and the fiery ranks,
　　 She reached the cherubim and her swiftness overtook the seraphim.
　　 Her course is directed to the Holy of Holies,[14] the interior one,[15]
　　 To the place of her Lord, Christ who is sitting at the right [hand of God].[16]
165　She entered the sanctuary[17] to see the Sublime in his place,
　　 His place is hidden, higher, and more exalted than creation.
　　 To [the place] where the Trinity is dwelling in its great glory,
　　 Faith hastened and entered and is not obstructed.
　　 Neither the minds nor the thoughts gaze upon her,
170　And not [even] the thoughts of the heavenly ones reach her.
　　 All the ranks of lofty beings fall short of her,
　　 And neither the legions nor the angels reach her.
　　 Created beings cannot approach her,
　　 For if fire were to climb there it would burn up immediately.

---

[13] Cf. Ephesians 6:12 and Colossians 1:16.
[14] Cf. Exodus 30:10.
[15] Cf. Hebrews 9:3.
[16] Cf. Colossians 3:1.
[17] Lit. "House of Holies."

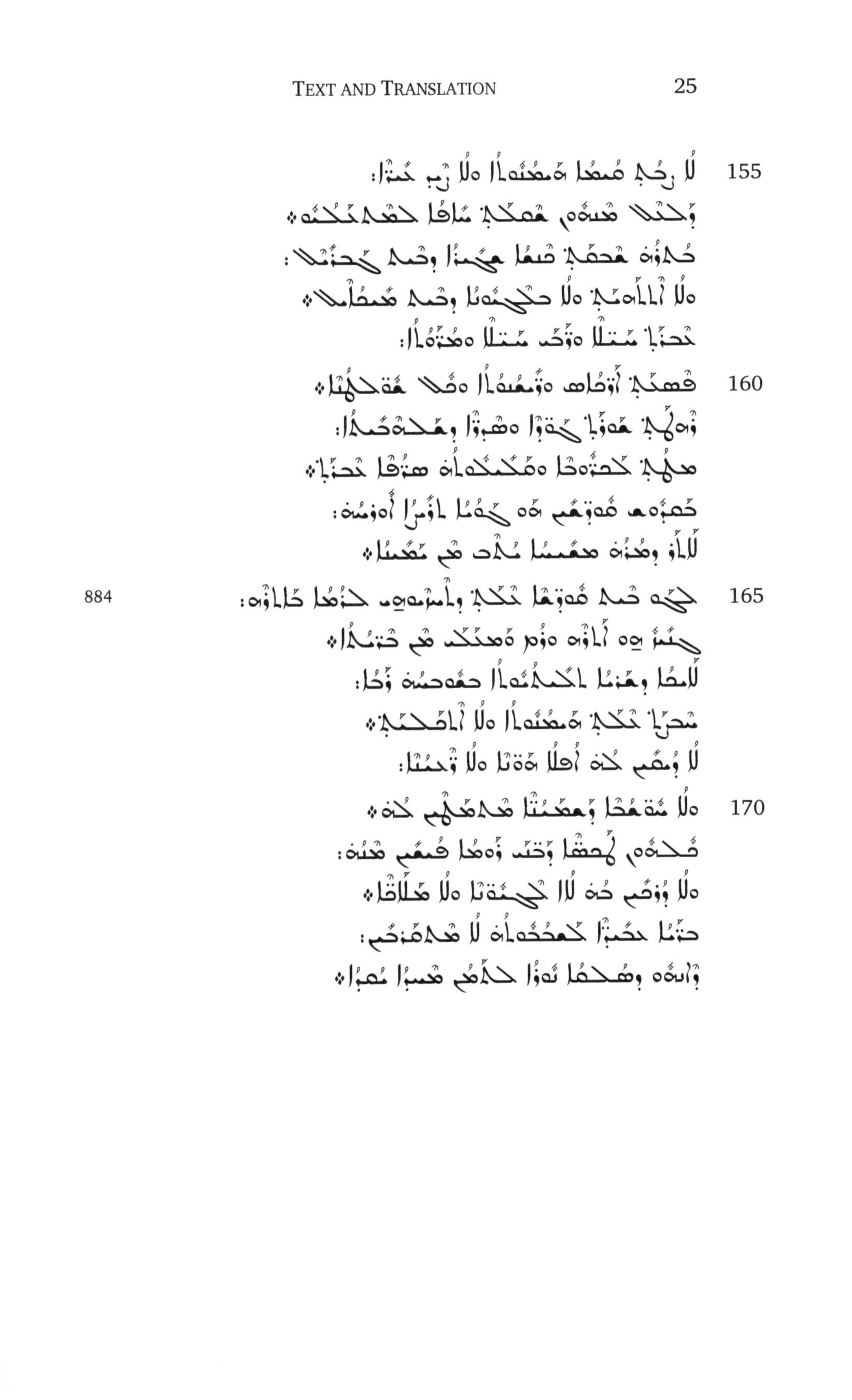

175 If the fiery assemblies of flames were brought near,
They would be nothing but chaff before a flame.
A fire blazes from the heavenly beings themselves,
But they cannot turn towards the Son.
The beings of flame drop burning coals,
180 But if they approach that place, they will burn up immediately.
The fearful cherubim whose lightning blazes from their wings,
Pour out holiness towards that place so that they do not burn up.[18]
The seraphim of fire conceals his face with his blazing wing,
So that he may not be singed by that place of the Godhead.[19]
185 Faith entered this place to see her Lord,
Where he is seated at the right hand of the hidden Father.[20]
The Son's place is the Father with the Holy Spirit,
The Trinity that is incomprehensible and ineffable.
"I shall sit here and take rest for I have longed for it,"
190 Faith says as it delights.
Hither be raised, come and see the place of faith,
For whoever was elevated to see her place has entered into repose.
The eye has not seen and the heart of man did not reckon,
What the Father prepared for those who love what is above.[21]

---

[18] Cf. Ezekiel 15:3.
[19] Cf. Isaiah 6:1–5.
[20] Cf. Colossians 3:1.
[21] Cf. 1 Corinthians 2:9.

175	:
	:
	:
180	
	:
	:
185	:
	:
	:
190	
	:
	:

885

195	Seek and consider the things above and do not seek for yourself
	The things that are below, which are nought but darkness.
	Whoever loves what is earthly and leaves what is above,
	His path is directed to the outer darkness.[22]
	The things of the earth drag you below the earth,
200	To a place of gloom and full of darkness for the one who descends to it.
	Beneath the earth is the outer darkness,
	And, behold, there is the lower Sheol of which David spoke.[23]
	This is the chasm that is full of darkness in which there is no brightness,
	And whoever falls into it, has no way to rise out from there.
205	Whoever falls until they land is unable to ascend,
	But if the one who fell lands, perhaps he can be raised.
	Because there is no bottom for that fall,
	[which is] everlasting and whoever has fallen did not reach the bottom.
	This is a chasm from which God Himself is remote,
210	And whoever falls within it, has nowhere to land.
	The power that holds the whole creation, is the very power carrying [the chasm],
	And [He] is not there, [so] where will the one who falls arrive?
	It is deprived light which neither descends to it, or shines into it,
	For if light descended there it would immediately be extinguished.

---

[22] Cf. Matthew 8:12.
[23] Cf. Psalm 86:13.

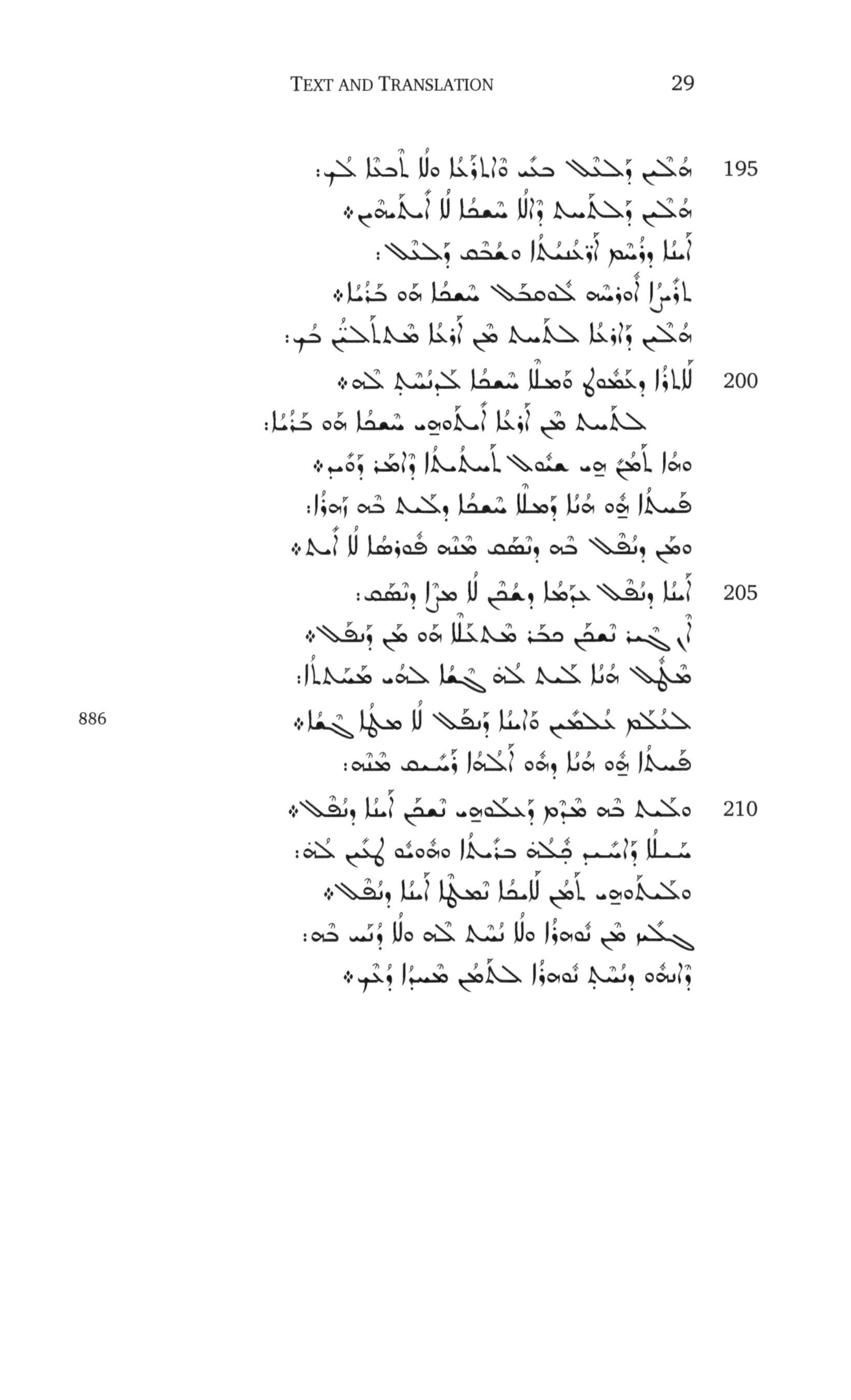

215 If myriads of suns were to descend to this place
     They would be nought but as the wick of a lamp.
     The Lord of light is not there, so which light
     Is able to descend and shine there without being corrupted?
     What is the place that is hidden away from God
220 If not the darkness? But woe to the person who is sent there!
     What can I say or what should I speak about that darkness?
     Its appearance is death and I don't know how to speak of it.
     God is far away from it and there is nothing for me to speak,
     Except woe unto whoever saw within it and beheld it.
225 All the heavenly orders tremble at it
     And shudder, quiver to turn their faces and gaze into it.
     Their Lord is remote from the place and they are shaken by it,
     For if their gaze inclines towards it, they will taste death.
     And since the moment the accuser[24] was cast down and fell there[25]
230 The whole assembly of the children of light are standing in fear.
     This is place of the Evil One and of his ministers
     For whoever practices iniquity and wickedness is sent to it.
     It is the place of the evil ones, and all the evil ones are sent to it,
     For they cast whoever has practiced iniquity and villainy into it.

---

[24] I.e., Satan.
[25] Cf. Luke 10:18.

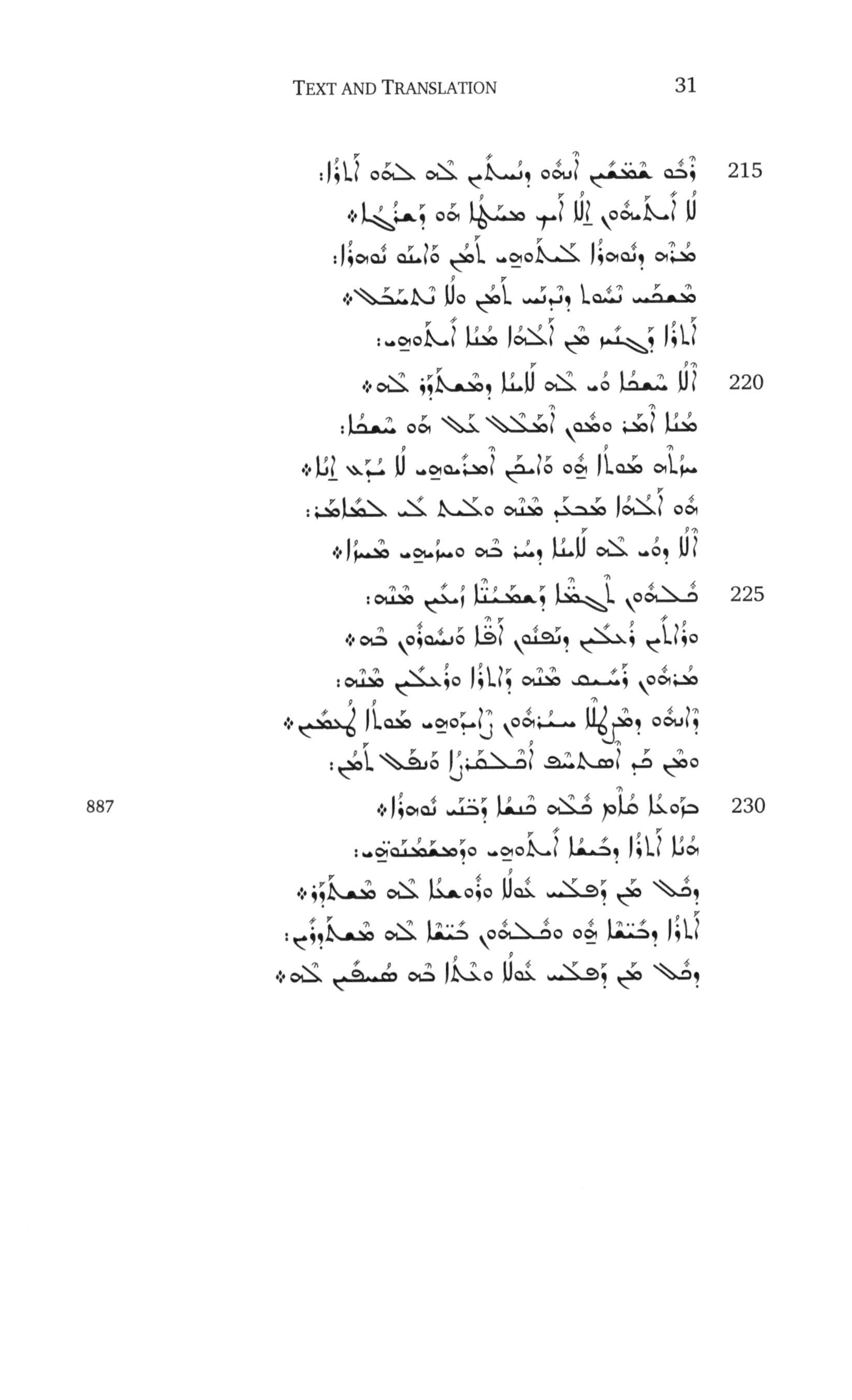

235	Burning mingles in that darkness in which there is no light,
	And the mouth has no means by which to speak of how it is.
	Behold, the adulterers and, behold, fornicators are cast there,
	For they have dishonored and corrupted the clean path of marriage.
	Behold, the plunderers and, behold, the avaricious ones cast there,
240	For they have oppressed, defrauded, and caused the needy and the poor to wail.
	He who gathered his wealth and filled his house with the belongings of others,
	The evil riches gathered nothing for him except darkness.
	He who loved deceit and possessed envy and evil passions,
	The sons of darkness do not envy him for he is with them.
245	He who took wealth, had an evil eye, and had no compassion
	To go and give daily bread to whoever was in need.
	The fiery abyss opens her mouth and receives him
	So that he descends and inherits that unending darkness.
	Whoever lived in luxury and was merry here like the rich man
250	There, asks for a drop of water and they do not grant it to him.[26]
	He whose pomp was puffed up, [who] deluded his companions, and treated his kin with contempt
	Is abased and miserable under the rule of the chief of evil.[27]
	Regarding he who stepped forward and transgressed the priest's word, and did not fear it,
	The earth and sky tremble at his torment.

---

[26] Cf. Luke 16:19–31.
[27] Cf. Isaiah 58:7.

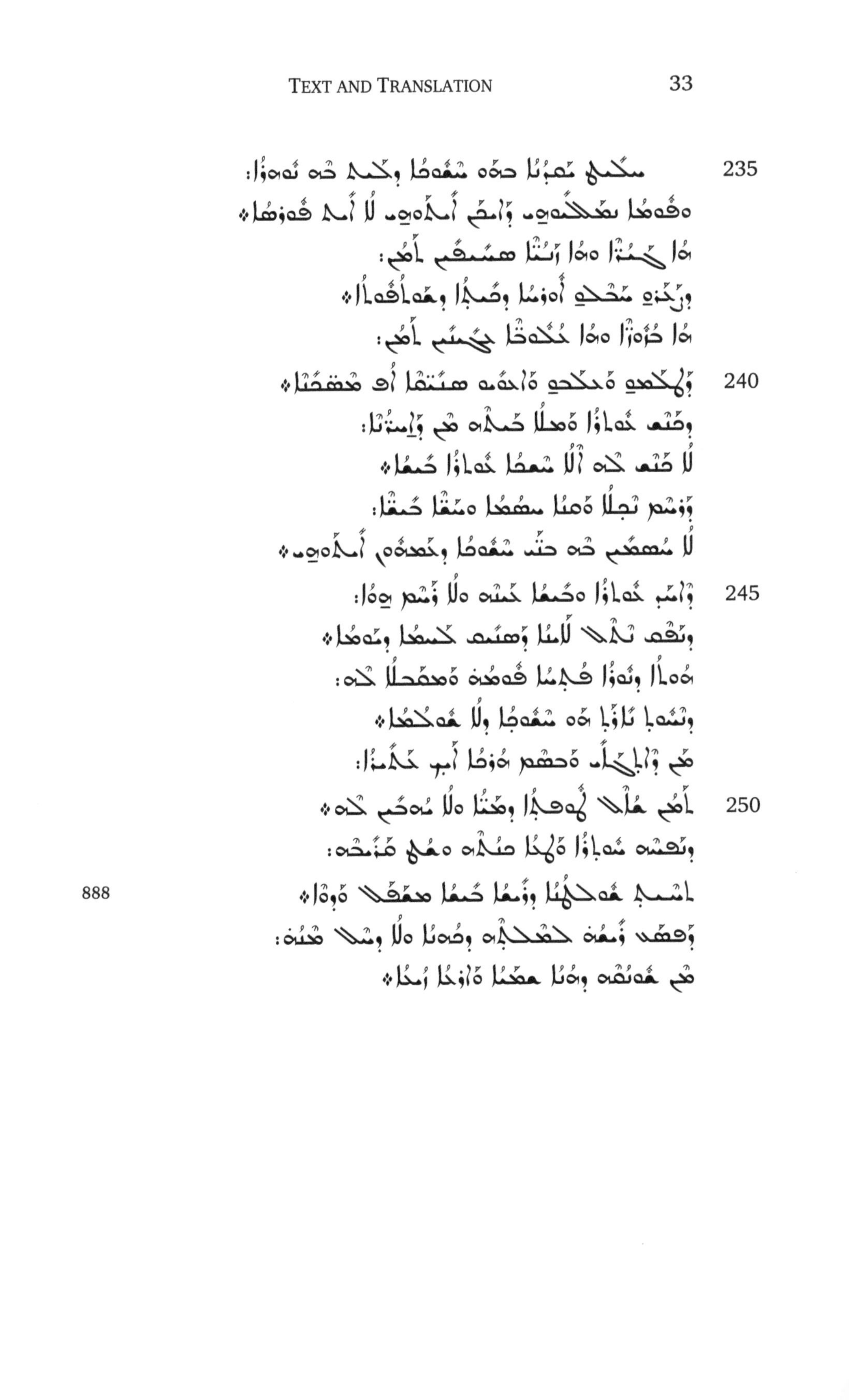

255 The one who defiled himself and corrupted his body with evil passions:
His hands and feet are bound and fettered and he is cast there.[28]
The one who got angry and pushed away love from himself to hate his brother,
That same chasm will be in a great reconciliation with him.
The mouth which pronounced all kinds of abuse and hateful speech
260 Will be quiet and silenced at that crying with great suffering.
The ear that loved to hear songs and jesting here,
The Evil One's tunes will be sung into it so that it becomes deaf.
The olfaction that loved the putrid scent of lasciviousness
Will be saddled by the foulness of impure demons there.
265 The eye that secretly gazed here
There, will be shut and full of darkness so that it will no longer see.
Whoever gave false testimony about their kin
Will be the companion of evil demons who taught him.
Woman whom the Evil One grabbed hold of[29] so that she looked at herself in the mirror,
270 Is shown frightful visions of all kinds of terrors.
Legs that wrongfully ran after theft
Will become limp and cast in the darkness for eternity.
The workers of iniquity are overthrown and cast down in the whirlpool,
And all unspeakable adversity surrounds them.

---

[28] Cf. Matthew 22:13.
[29] Bedjan's footnote, *encouraged*.

TEXT AND TRANSLATION

275	A shout rises from the darkness but there is no one to answer,
	And there is weeping but no deliverer and no help.
	The thundering of the cries of suffering which rend rocks rise,
	And the door of despair is closed [on them] by the judge.
	Mercy is withheld and wrath is issued onto the unruly,
280	And the mouth of the fiery chasm is closed upon the impious.
	Because they held the Son of God's commandments in contempt,
	And did not heed [them], whenever they call to him, they will not be heard.
	They increase their cries but there is no one to answer nor even listen,
	And justice closes the door and does not open it.
285	Wrath closed the door of mercy in the face of the wicked,
	And however much they cry out, [their] affliction increases and they are not heard.
	Here the door of mercy is open before sinners,
	And it is easy for you to enter each day if you wish.
	Behold, grace opens the door and calls to the wicked
290	To come, enter and take shelter from justice with her.
	Seek mercy for yourself before the door is closed in front of you,
	And you increase your cries when there is no one to answer or hear you.
	See how the prophet David prostrated himself,
	And beseeching mercy from God with great passion.

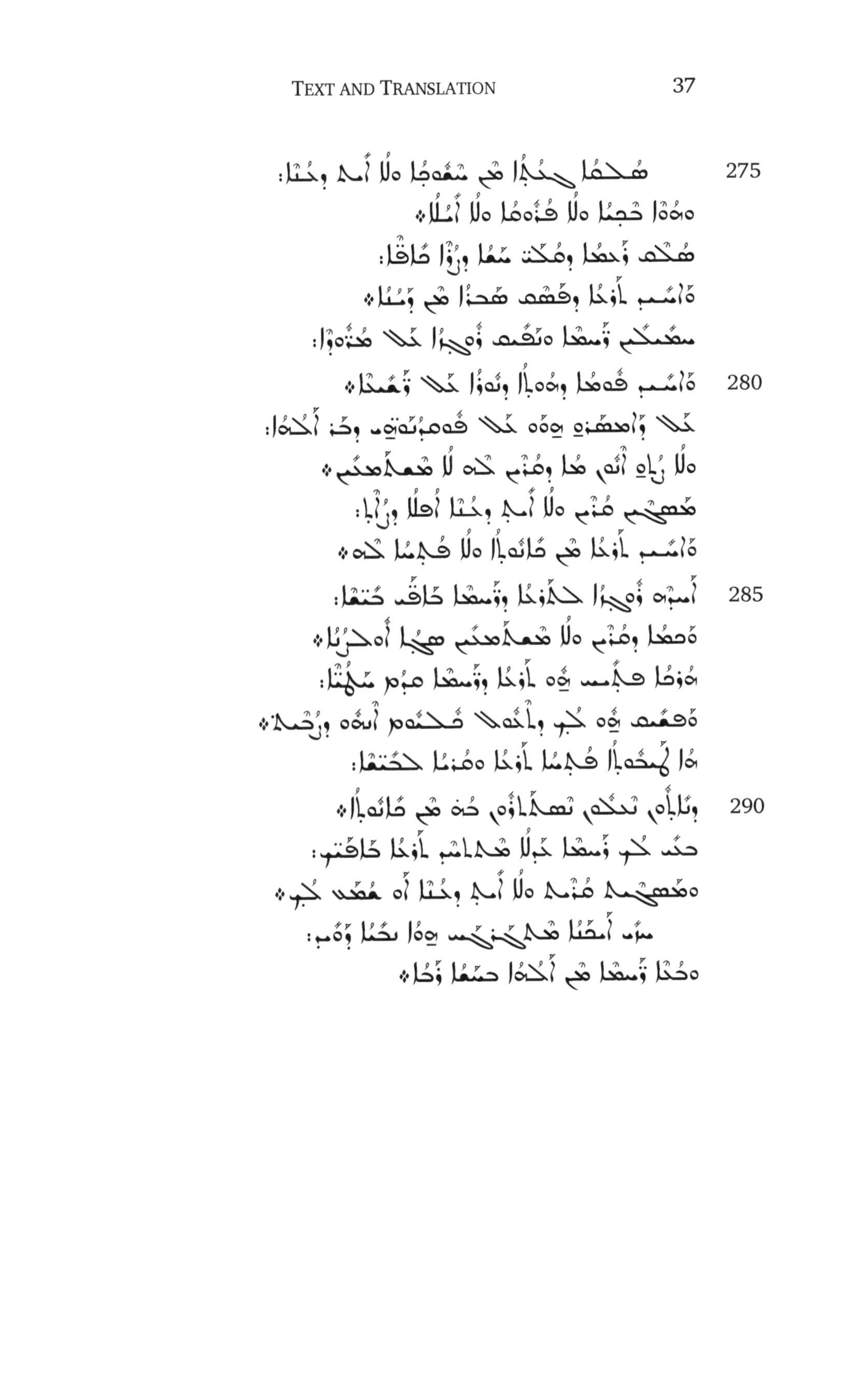

295 In the nights, his bed was moistened with tears,
And his bedding was dampened by his eyes. [30]
His eyes were grieved by frequent, daily crying,
And because of the eye's trickle, its color waned.
Lord, my God, by the abundance of your mercy, answer your servant,
300 Also, by the bounty of your salvation Lord, save me. [31]
So that I may not go down to [the chasm], from that foul mire of demons,
And from the whirlpool filled with sin, you, my Lord, save me.
May the fearful chasm filled with darkness not swallow me,
And may the bottomless pit of its mouth not seize me.
305 Answer me, God, in accordance with your mercy and your grace,
And by the abundance of your compassion Lord, save me.
Lord, turn towards the miserable, infirm soul,
And do not deliver it to the adversaries who despise humankind.
May the endless mercies come towards me,
310 May they bring me towards the salvation that shines from you.
Save me from the evil deeds of my enemies, O Lord,
Behold, they entice me to descend with them into the darkness.
My Lord, I am your image, may the sons of perdition not deride me,
And may they not say about me: Aha, aha, our eye has seen him. [32]

---

[30] Cf. Psalm 6:6–7.
[31] Cf. Psalm 69:13, 16.
[32] Cf. Psalm 35:21.

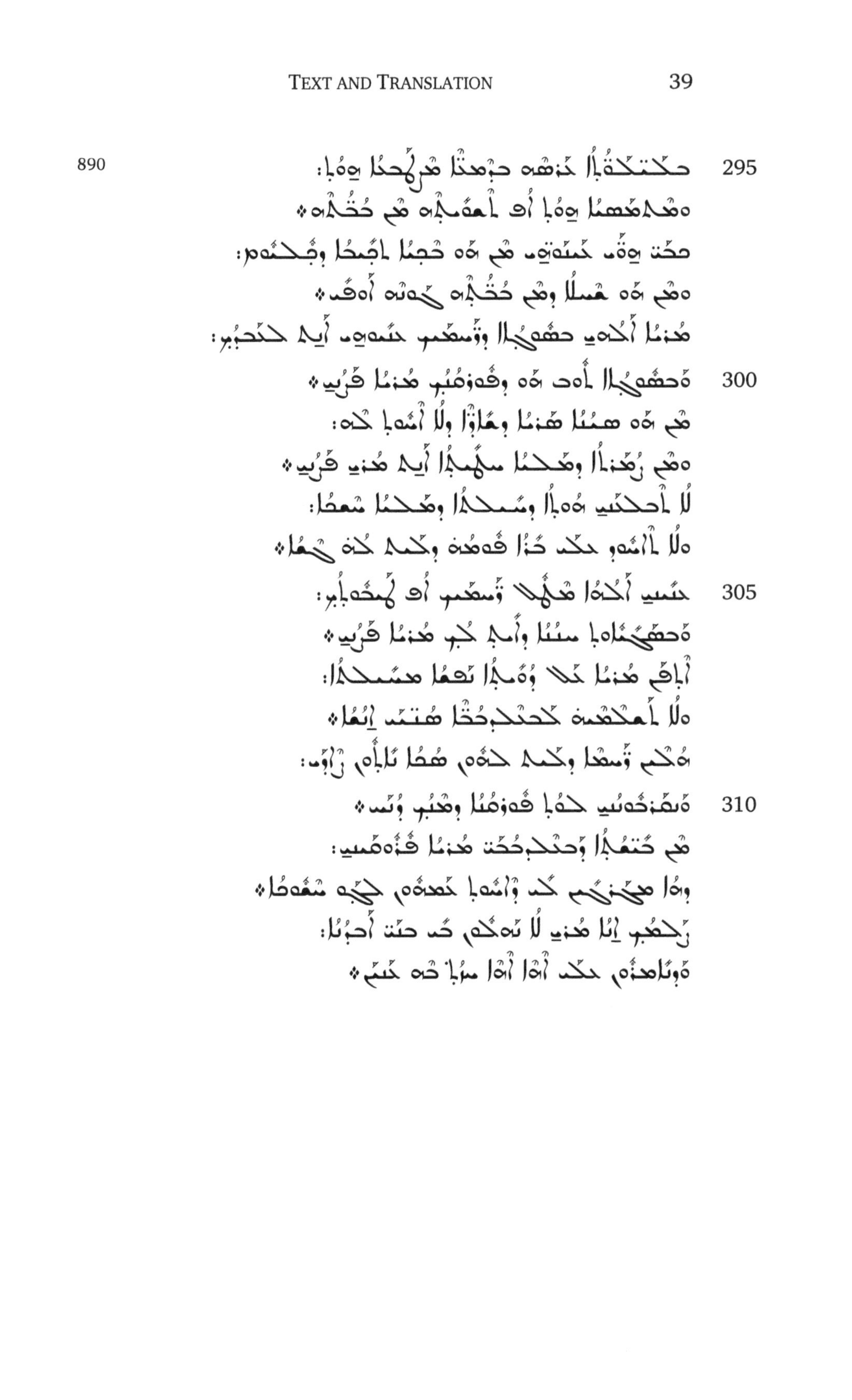

890

315 Were I to descend to the darkness, there would be no gain,
For dust in Sheol neither gives you thanks nor glorifies you.[33]
You are not praised by the dead who descend to Sheol,[34]
None of those who are in darkness give you thanks.[35]
You are blessed by the lofty beings and the earthly beings,
320 And by the penitent who come towards you to repent.
Take tears from the sinners for yourself and grant [them] forgiveness,
And receive my groaning as that of Job and absolve my sins.[36]
Behold, I am mixing the tears of my eyes with [my] drink of water,[37]
I will drink them and wash the sins of [my] soul in them.
325 Because there is none among the living who is blameless or justified before you,[38]
Let your mercy petition on behalf of sinners in the court.[39]
May your compassion enter and be an advocate in place of my guilt,
And may [it] defend me, beseeching these [words].
This wretch is nothing and nor are his sins;
330 Lord, do not bring him to judgement before you.
A drop of mercy from that infinite sea,
Is able to wash the iniquities of the world if you so will it.
You do not desire to hinder [your] mercy from sinners,
It is [their choice] to hinder mercy, for they did not seek mercy.

---

[33] Cf. Psalm 115:17 and 6:6.
[34] Ibid.
[35] Cf. Psalm 6:6 and Isaiah 38:18.
[36] Cf. Job 23:2.
[37] Cf. Psalm 102:9.
[38] Cf. Psalm 143:2 and 51:4.
[39] Lit. "house of judgement."

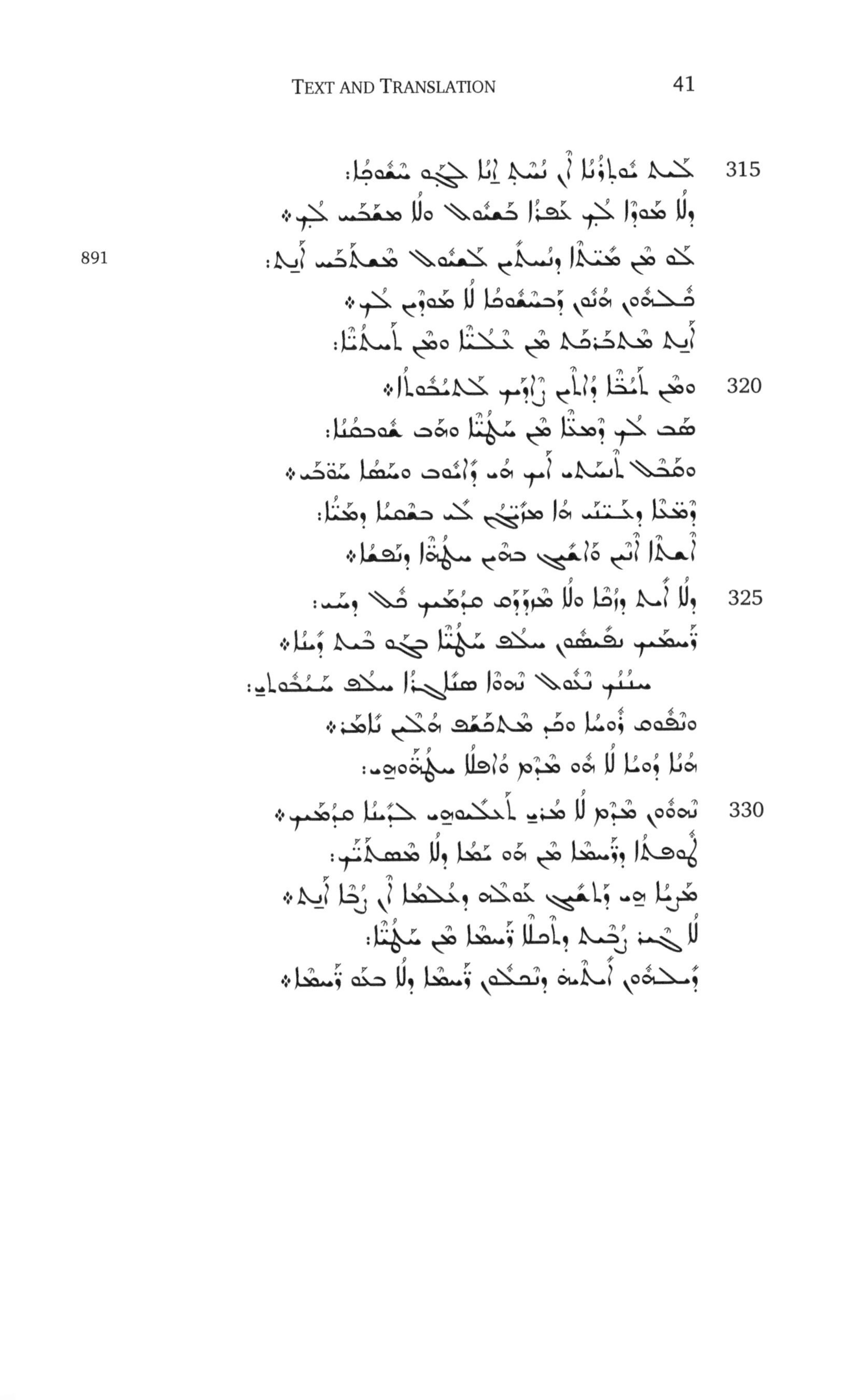

891

335   Your mercy is overflowing, your love spread, and your door opened,
And your hands are extended, embracing whoever repents.
That younger son[40] who went far from you and returned towards you,
You fell upon his neck and he was embraced by your kisses.[41]
When he went to a place remote from your will
340   And dissipated his goods on harlots and lechery.[42]
But as soon as he repented, came to his sense, and confessed that he sinned
and poured out tears, he was received with mercy and love.
Oh, Good One, whose door of mercy is opened and [who] invites the wicked,
Glory to you and mercy on us at all times.

---

[40] Cf. Luke 15:11–30.
[41] Luke 15:20.
[42] Luke 15:30.

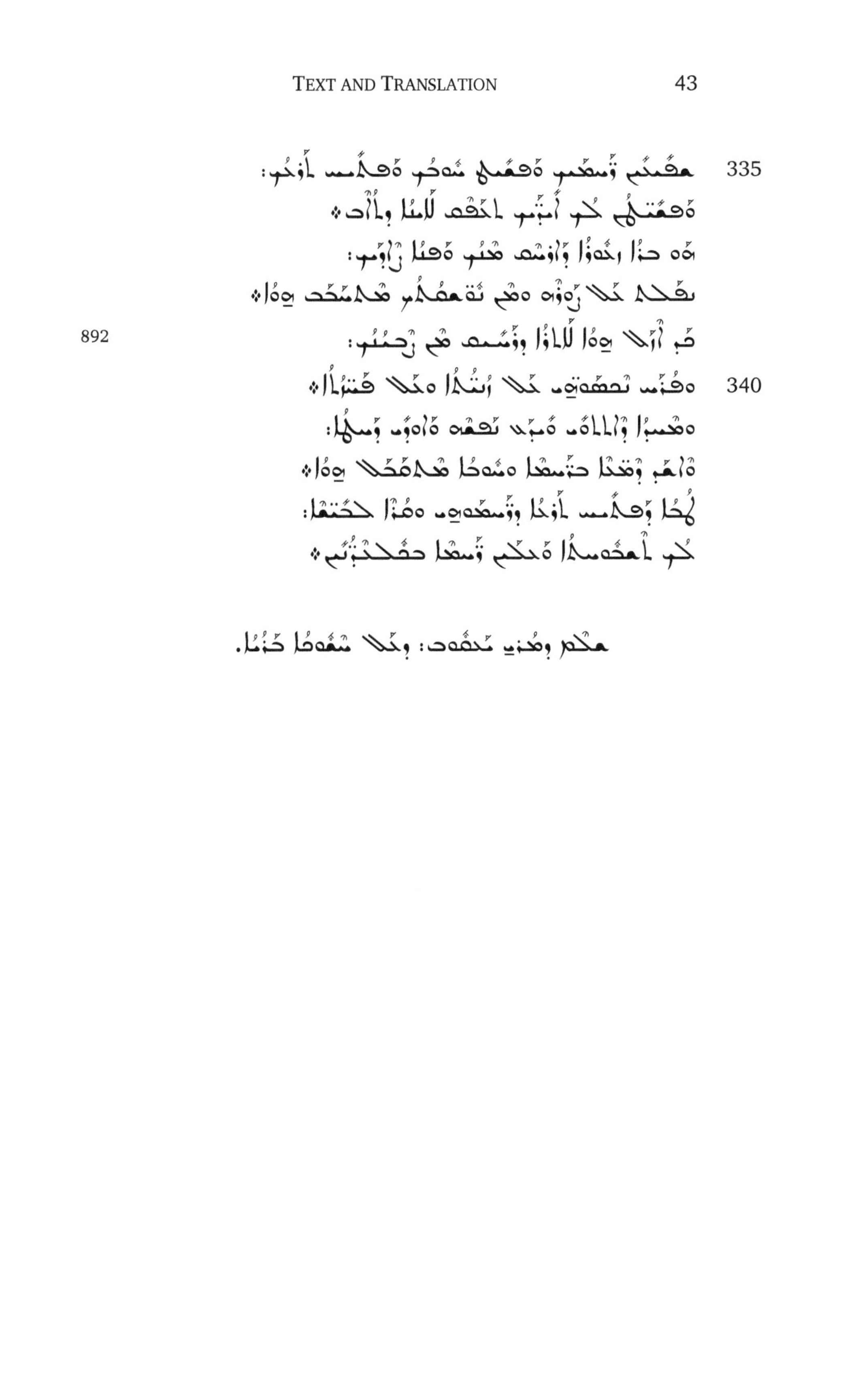

BIBLIOGRAPHY

Brock, Sebastian. "An Early Maronite text on Prayer." *Parole de l'Orient* 13 (1986): 79–94.

Brock, Sebastian. *The Harp of the Spirit: Poems of Saint Ephrem the Syrian.* Cambridge: Aquila Books, 2013.

Harvey, Susan Ashbrook. "To Whom Did Jacob Preach?" In *Jacob of Serugh and His Times: Studies in Sixth-Century Syriac Christianity*, edited by George Kiraz, 115–132. Piscataway: Gorgias Press, 2010.

Saber, George. "La Typologie Sacramentaire et Baptismale de Saint Ephrem." *Parole de l'Orient* 5, no. 1–2 (1973): 73–91.

INDEX OF BIBLICAL REFERENCES

References are to line number

Exodus		Isaiah	
30:10	161	6:1–5	184
		38:18	318
Numbers		42:5a	14
3	40	40:22	142
		58:7	252
Job			
23:2	322	Ezekiel	
		15:3	182
Psalms			
6:6–7	296, 316, 318	Matthew	
19:1	6	7:19	113
20	74, 78	8:12	198
35:21	314	22:13	256
49:12	74, 78		
52:8	111	Luke	
52:5	113	3:9	113
51:4	325	10:18	229
69:13	300	15:11–30	337
69:16	314	15:20	338
80:12–13	80	15:30	340
86:13	202	16:19–31	250
92:12	112		
102:9	323	1 Corinthians	
115:17	316	2:9	194
143:2	325		

Ephesians
  6:12   160

Colossians
  1:16   160
  3:1   145, 164, 186
  3:2   150

Hebrews
  9:3   161

www.ingramcontent.com/pod-product-compliance
Ingram Content Group UK Ltd.
Pitfield, Milton Keynes, MK11 3LW, UK
UKHW021305180426
11947UKWH00015B/1022